When Your Long-Term Pastor
Leaves Your Church

When Your Long-Term Pastor Leaves Your Church

Successfully Navigating a Unique Ministry Transition

Larry A. Gilpin

First Edition: 2016

Printed in the United States of America

ISBN: 978-0-9965168-5-3

Great Writing Publications
www.greatwriting.org
Taylors, SC,
in association with

DISCIPLESHIP MINISTRIES

www.pcacdm.org
1-800-283-1357

In This Book. . .

The time of transition following the tenure of a long-term pastor is a unique season in the life of a congregation. However, the distinct elements and potential difficulties of these transitions can be overcome—these transitions can work! Churches can navigate this season of ministry with the confidence that God can facilitate a successful transition process. *When Your Long-Term Pastor Leaves Your Church* describes, through a survey of biblical narratives as well as through more current real-life examples, the different ways churches go through transitions after a long-term pastor—with good, bad, or mixed results. The book then discusses ways a congregation, its pastors, elders, and pastoral search committee can safeguard against a poor transition and promote one that is successful. It provides practical guidance for churches that not only want to prevent a problematic transition after a long-term pastor, but want to actually promote one that works.

Appreciations

Larry Gilpin brings a wealth of pastoral experience with many examples to help churches understand issues that they will face during pastoral transitions. The time lines and checklists at the end of the book are particularly helpful for search committees seeking to understand and organize their responsibilities.

Bryan Chapell, Grace Presbyterian Church (PCA), Peoria, Illinois
President Emeritus, Covenant Theological Seminary

Pastoral transitions are difficult even in the healthiest of churches. Larry has drawn from personal experience and research. But he also carefully studied the experience of three very different congregations transitioning from long-term pastorates. Regardless of the circumstances, every congregational search committee and Session seeking a new pastor would greatly benefit from a thoughtful review of his work.

Robert W. Burns, Assistant Pastor, Seven Hills Fellowship (PCA), Rome, Georgia; Adjunct Professor of Educational Ministries, Covenant Theological Seminary

Love for the Bride of Christ demands gospel-centered transitions by pastors and local church leaders. Written by a journeyman pastor who has navigated the dangerous waters of several pastoral transitions, *When Your Long-Term Pastor Leaves*

Your Church is a must read for every search committee, ruling board, and pastor (because every pastor is a "departing pastor"). Not only can I recommend a book I have personally found helpful, I can commend Larry Gilpin as an author who is a dear friend whom I have watched practice what he preaches out of love for Jesus and by His grace.

George Robertson, Senior Pastor, First Presbyterian Church (PCA), Augusta, Georgia

I am delighted to recommend this well-researched work by Dr. Larry Gilpin on the church's practice of healthy pastoral transition after a relatively long pastorate. My observation is that the majority of search committees choose the wrong successor and therefore he becomes an "Unintentional Interim" lasting no longer than four to seven years. In the process, great damage is inflicted upon the church—as well as on the pastor and his family. Dr. Gilpin provides invaluable counsel regarding general principles and effective procedures useful for finding a successor who will lead the church into many years of God-honoring ministry.

Philip D. Douglass, Professor of Applied Theology, Covenant Theological Seminary

This book will be a great resource to help churches going through a transition in leadership, especially when a long serving pastor departs. The author wisely begins with biblical examples of leadership transition: Moses, David, Jesus, and Paul. He then offers realistic case studies of churches which have gone through leadership transitions with varying degrees of success. Finally, the practical principles for all those affected by transition (incoming pastor, outgoing pastor, search committee, congregation, lay leadership) are helpfully summarized at the end of the book. I consider that this will be a very helpful resource for our local church, which I helped to start over twenty-five years ago, as the people there deal with my departure to a new ministry situation.

Jim Newheiser, Director of the Christian Counseling Program at Reformed Theological Seminary, Charlotte, North Carolina; Executive Director of IBCD

I'm so thankful for my friend Larry Gilpin's book on long-term ministry transitions. I just wish my church family could have had it four years ago when I was making my transition off the Christ Community Church staff. As a founding pastor with a twenty-six year tenure, I found new meaning in singing the line from *Amazing Grace*, "Through many dangers, toils and snares we have already come." Indeed, long-term transitions can be very difficult, for congregation and pastor alike. Ours went remarkably well, but not without its hitches. This is why I'm excited to endorse and celebrate Larry's contribution to this very important conversation. Every church should have a copy, not only for themselves, but also as a way of knowing how to pray for other congregations entering a season of pastoral transition.

Dr. Scotty Smith, Teacher in Residence at West End Community Church, Nashville Tennessee, and Founding Pastor of Christ Community Church, Franklin Tennessee

In the life of every congregation, change is inevitable and sometimes difficult. A change of pastor, particularly a long-term pastor, is a unique challenge because of the myriad of emotions, expectations, and potential points of conflict. That is why this book is so helpful. In these pages, Larry Gilpin provides a helpful tool for those attempting to maneuver through the maze of a pastoral transition. By analyzing and extracting principles from actual situations, he equips leaders to ask good questions and make wise decisions. This book is a must read for pastors considering a move, as well as any leader who wants to help the congregation respond well to change.

Stephen Estock, Coordinator, PCA Discipleship Ministries

Dedication

To Corley: Thank you for faithfully modeling the love, grace, compassion, and commitment of Jesus to me and our family. Truly, "You excel them all." (Proverbs 31:29)

Acknowledgments

Even with a relatively short book, there are numerous people to thank. No book ever gets written or published merely by one's own efforts. So, I offer my sincere thanks: to Bob Burns, who first recommended I write this book. To my sister, Betsy, both for her consistent encouragement and her initial editing. To Jim Holmes, for his great support and editorial work. This project would not have happened without your involvement—thank you for helping me see that it was actually possible. To my mother-in-law, Annette, who prays faithfully for my ministry. To the Fellowship Presbyterian Church in Newport, Tennessee, the Monroeville Presbyterian Church in Monroeville, Alabama, and the Westminster Presbyterian Church in Martinez, Georgia, for allowing me to be your pastor. To the many friends who have taken an interest in this project and have asked about its progress. To my wife, Corley, and my daughters, Emily and Lauren—for loving me and for making home and family a place of refuge and enjoyment for me. And to the God of all grace—that He truly loves me in Christ and is *for* me both in life and ministry. May He use this book to bless His church. To Him be the glory!

Table of Contents

A Note about Terms

This book is written with my background and church association being a Presbyterian one. Some of the terms used are fairly distinctive to my church affiliation—such as "Session" (the local governing body of elders in a Presbyterian church), "Diaconate" (the body of deacons in a Presbyterian church) and "Presbytery" (the regional governing body of ministers and congregations in a Presbyterian church). In addition, some of the processes for selecting a pastor are distinctive to my own affiliation. However, I believe readers from any church, whatever its form of government or specific means of securing a pastor may be, will benefit from considering the biblical concepts and the issues related to transitions addressed in this book.

Also, the *focus* of this book is on transitions after a long-term pastor. However, the material can be useful for *any* pastoral transition—whether it occurs after many years or after a relatively brief pastoral tenure. Any pastoral transition is a time of great significance in a congregation. I believe the principles set forth in this book will help churches face that season of ministry with greater clarity and insight.

Pastoral Transitions:

~~~

Times of Ecstasy or Agony?

Michael served as pastor of Gracewood Presbyterian Church for almost fifteen years. His tenure was the longest ever at the church and was marked by consistent, though not spectacular, growth in numbers. His congregation appreciated his preaching, pastoral skills, and the steadiness he provided. He and his elders occasionally disagreed on issues facing the congregation. However, this did not hinder his faithfulness in ministry to the church, nor the mutual love he and his elders had for one another. He resigned to accept a call to a congregation in another state that had been through a time of deep conflict, believing his pastoral skills were needed there.

He was replaced by Robert, who was fourteen years younger than his predecessor and is now in his ninth year of ministry at Gracewood. Previously, Robert was an assistant pastor for four years at a much larger congregation. Gracewood is his first solo pastorate. Due to needs and available funds as a result of increased numerical growth over the past four years, Gracewood has built a new fellowship hall and educational wing. Though Robert was young when he came to the church, even the older members have related well to him and have enjoyed their interaction with him, his wife, and their young children. And although the congregation has a quiet apprehension that Robert will one day be called to a larger church, for the moment its members are enjoying his ministry and hope it continues.

* * *

Al was the senior pastor of Rivermont Presbyterian Church for just over ten years. During his tenure, the church grew in members and staff and financial giving was consistently high. He was loved deeply by his congregation and highly respected in his community. He could state his understanding of Scripture on the most controversial topics in a very personable way. Even those in the church who sometimes disagreed with him still were supportive of his ministry and enjoyed being around him. He was, in many ways, the quintessential pastor-teacher.

His congregation was heartbroken when he announced he was resigning to become pastor of a different church in another part of the country. One observer said "everyone cried" on his last Sunday. After he was gone, a pastoral search committee was formed, and its members began to look for Al's replacement. The committee did not take a long time to complete its work. Six months later it recommended Dave, a man slightly younger than Al, and the congregation called him as its new pastor. Though Dave had strengths, he was somewhat hard to get to know, and some staff members found it difficult to work with him. During the first six months of his tenure, two key staff persons began looking for other positions. In addition, in the terms of one elder, he "ran off" a third staff member. Relational problems with staff, officers, and other members of the congregation continued throughout his tenure. After two years he was asked by his Session (the leadership group for churches in his denomination) to begin seeking another place of ministry. He resigned about a month after this request.

* * *

Ray was fifty-four years old when he was called as pastor of Springdale Presbyterian Church and stayed until his retirement eleven years later. He came to the church after the founding pastor left. His tenure was marked by relative peace in the church, though not by high levels of numerical growth. His members thought he balanced his teaching-preaching and "people" responsibilities well. He was succeeded by Jeff, a forty-year-old man with about fourteen years of ministry experience. He has been at Springdale now for two years. Many people feel the transition went well and that the change was mostly positive. Jeff has made some changes which have annoyed some elders but which have been well received by others. Some members of the congregation have left the church, unhappy with the "new direction" under Jeff. Yet, others feel they have grown spiritually in ways they have never grown before, and they give credit for this to Jeff's sound teaching. Those who support him—actually a solid majority of the congregation—are very strong in their support and would be disappointed if he were to leave. Yet, a small minority of members would not be terribly disappointed if he were to move on.

While these three scenarios aren't direct accounts of specific pastoral transitions, they are representative of typical events that occur when a long-term pastor leaves his congregation. Sometimes that transition goes well; sometimes it goes quite poorly; at other times the results are mixed.

The Elephant

Pastoral placement has been described as "matchmaking" that can be "an ecstasy of opportunity or an agony of decision."[1] Transitions from one pastor to another also have been referred to as "the elephant in the boardroom"—something big and threatening—which people pretend isn't there or don't want to talk about.[2] Yet if people don't talk—in advance of, during and after—about these transitions, the church suffers. The reality is that every pastor is a departing pastor—and churches need to prepare for the inevitable and eventual time of transition they will face.

Maintaining Biblical Priorities

Yet, mere preparation is not enough—we need to think and act biblically amid these transitions. We see the preparation for leadership transition in Acts 20, where Paul addressed the elders in Ephesus as he was about to depart from them. He emphasized the biblical pastoral priorities of public and private ministry (v. 20) and of proclaiming the entirety of God's word (v. 27). He emphasized the responsibility of elders to guard the spiritual welfare of God's people (v. 28) and set forth the sufficiency of the Lord and His word—to which Paul entrusted for safekeeping those who had been under his care (v. 32). Good transitions in pastoral leadership are not simply a matter of following human wisdom, but involve a dependence on the grace of God and a biblically shaped approach to the ministry of Christ's church.

What Makes Long-Term Transitions Unusual?

Yet, as we pursue biblical priorities, we need to understand our ministry context, and the context of replacing a long-term pastor has unique dynamics. First of all, transitions after a long-term pastor are unusual, whether the pastor leaves amid amicable conditions or in the midst of circumstances that have been more tumultuous. A long-term pastorate itself isn't common in contemporary American churches, where pastoral transitions occur frequently. The average pastor in America has served in his pastorate for five years.[3] In my own denomination, the Presbyterian Church in America (PCA), the average pastoral stay as a solo or senior pastor is seven and one-third years.[4] So, the transition from a long-term pastor who has served at least ten years provides a much more unusual situation for a congregation. The figure of ten years, though admittedly arbitrary, is a realistic figure for defining a long-term pastorate in the PCA, since the average pastoral tenure in the denomination is just over seven years.

Lots of Variables

In addition, a church's process of pastoral transition after a relatively long pastorate involves a lot of variables including the personalities, spiritual gifts, and leadership styles of the former pastor and the successor pastor; the expectations or desires of the leadership of the congregation regarding the successor pastor; the grounds for congregational "acceptance" of the successor pastor; the quality of relationships the former pastor had with members of the congregation; and the goals of the successor pastor for the congregation and the manner in which he pursues them. Certainly these factors can be present in any pastoral transition, but their weight may be increased when a pastor has had a relatively long tenure and is being succeeded by someone new.

In these unique circumstances for a pastoral transition, what makes the difference in the ultimate results? Do things just happen with little explanation, or are there particular factors or dynamics in a transition scenario that contribute to the success or lack of success of the transition? In particular, can a congregation, its elders and its pastoral search committee engage in a specific course of action to safeguard against a poor transition and to promote one that is successful? The answer is "yes!" The more important issue is, "How can it happen?" First of all, as churches seek to promote a healthy transition, they can be helped by looking at some of the leadership transitions the Bible describes.

Practical Questions for Consideration

1. What are some personal qualities that make your long-term pastor unique and appreciated by your congregation?

2. What are the ministry areas in which your long-term pastor is clearly gifted? What are areas of ministry in which he is not particularly strong?

3. What are some dynamics or variables that you see in your own congregation that could make a transition after your long-term pastor difficult?

4. Are there persons in your congregation who have experience in a pastoral search (whether it occurred in your congregation or somewhere else)?

-2-

Biblical Examples of
Leadership Transition

The Bible itself addresses the topic of leadership transition. While it doesn't set forth a fully developed theology of ministerial transition or a clear model for transition following a spiritual leader of long tenure, Scripture does provide several examples in which one spiritual leader succeeded another. In some cases, the previous leader had served for many years. These transitions resulted in different outcomes, with the succeeding leader attaining varying levels of success and acceptance by God's people.

Old Testament Examples

The leadership transitions in the Old Testament often occurred through family descent, as in the case of kings. In other cases God clearly designated the successor leader. However the transitions occurred, they provide examples of how preparation for transition affected the success which followed.

Moses led the Israelites for forty years then prepared for the transition of that leadership role to Joshua. In Deuteronomy 31, Moses affirms what God would do for His people so that they could take possession of the land of Canaan, and He charges Joshua with responsibilities of leadership of the people (vs. 1-8). Whether these verses are complete accounts or summary statements, preparation for leadership transition was made and the transition apparently went smoothly, based on the material we find in the book of Joshua.[5] God Himself affirms Joshua's succession of Moses in leadership,[6] concluding a process that had begun as God instructed Moses to select Joshua as his successor years earlier.[7]

In this transition, "keys to Joshua's success seem to lie in his extensive preparation for the task, Moses' commendation of Joshua to the people, Joshua's deep commitment to obeying and relying upon God, and God's choice to raise up Joshua as a leader."[8] Moses' commendation provided a degree of connection between himself and Joshua in relation to the Israelites and was an important factor in allowing the people to trust their new leader.

Another key leadership transition in Scripture occurred as David was succeeded as king by his son Solomon. Just as Moses made preparation for someone to succeed him in leadership of the Israelites, David also made preparation for his son Solomon to succeed him as king.[9] He charges Solomon to "keep the charge of the Lord your God, walking in his ways and keeping his statutes, his commandments, his rules, and his testimonies, as it is written in the Law of Moses, that you may prosper in all that you do and wherever you turn, that the Lord may establish his word that he spoke concerning me, saying, 'If your sons pay close attention to their way, to walk before me in faithfulness with all their heart and with all their soul, you shall not lack a man on the throne of Israel.'"[10] There was an attempt to keep Solomon from the position of king in Israel,[11] and he later put potential rivals to death.[12] Nevertheless, the transition resulted in a long-term reign for Solomon. However, Solomon's idolatry ultimately incurred the judgment of God, specifically the eventual division of the Israelite kingdom into two separate kingdoms, Israel and Judah.[13] The transition of spiritual leadership—though it may begin well— does not always end with good results.

The story of Elijah and Elisha, recorded in 2 Kings 2:1-18, provides another primary biblical example of leadership transition. Here, the literal mantel of leadership was passed from Elijah to Elisha, whom God had instructed Elijah to anoint as prophet in Elijah's place (1 Kings 19:15–16). Elijah indicated that he would be taken from Elisha, and Elisha asked for a "double portion" of Elijah's spirit. This request was granted by God when, as chariots of fire and horses of fire separated the two prophets, Elijah went up by a whirlwind into heaven. While the passage may be more descriptive than prescriptive, it nevertheless shows God's provision for leadership transition among His people.

New Testament Examples

The New Testament also contains several examples of ministry transition. While Jesus' position is a unique, non-repeatable one, He nevertheless made preparation for His own transition from His earthly ministry to His ascension into heaven. He told His disciples, "Yet a little while I am with you "[14] and emphasized that He was telling them ahead of time that He would be leaving the earth.[15] He also reminded the disciples that though He was going away, He would send the Holy Spirit to be with them.[16] He instructed them as to what their responsibilities would be once He had returned to heaven.[17]

Paul made several transitions to new leaders during his ministry in the early church. He prepared Timothy for future ministry by allowing Timothy to spend significant amounts of time traveling with him (see Acts 16:1-5). Paul's two letters to Timothy also show his investment of wisdom with Timothy, as he instructed him how to continue the ministry of the church to which Paul himself had been devoted.

As mentioned in the previous chapter, Paul also gave instructions to the elders in Ephesus as he transitioned from ministry among them (see Acts 20:17-32). He recounted the things he had done with them and warned them of false teachers who would seek to lead the church astray. He gave specific responsibilities related to their spiritual care of God's people and committed these leaders to God's care.

An additional ministry transition—from Paul to Apollos—occurred in Corinth. Paul was the spiritual father of the Corinthian church and Apollos continued the ministry of the gospel there. Paul, though brilliant intellectually, was perhaps not rhetorically refined and spoke with simplicity.[18] Although Apollos was different from Paul in terms of speaking style and message presentation, there was no fundamental difference in the two men's message; they proclaimed the same gospel. Yet, in both 1 Corinthians chapters 1 and 3, Paul addresses a misdirected focus among the church, whose attention was off of Christ and instead directed at individual leaders. The emphasis on personal preference for particular leaders instead of on Christ demonstrated a degree of spiritual immaturity on the part of the church amid ministry transition.

Paul also describes the qualifications for elders in 1 Timothy 3:1-13 and Titus 1:5-8. In addition, Peter gives instruction to elders in 1 Peter 5:1-4. Each passage is applicable to leadership transition in the local church. 1 Timothy and Titus were written so that the early church would know whom to select as its officers. These verses also would provide guidance to established congregations as they would seek to identify potential new leaders and to determine spiritual suitability for leadership. The 1 Peter passage was written to Christians in more established church situations, and again Jesus is making provision for transition in His church.

While the examples of Elijah and Elisha, David and Solomon, and Moses and Joshua may not actually be set forth as biblical *norms* for leadership transition, they certainly provide *examples* of how transitions took place among God's people. In addition, though the transitions from one king to another occurred *primarily* through family descent, they are instructive as well, in that some of them show a degree of preparation for transition and an evaluation of how well transitions succeeded. Since the New Testament says that "whatever was written in former days [i.e., in the Old Testament] was written for our instruction,"[19] these examples should in some measure inform our understanding of the transition of leaders among God's people. Also, the New Testament's focus on qualifications for officers and the church's attitudes toward its ministers shows God's concern for the transitions that occur in the spiritual leadership of His people and His desire that those transitions go well.

Just as the results of transitions recorded in Scripture are varied, pastoral transitions have a variety of outcomes today. We can gain some important insights as to how—or how not—to approach these transitions by looking at what occurred in some current day congregations when they replaced their long-term pastor. In the pages following, we'll look at three churches and their experience of transition after a pastor had served ten years or more. These examples bring to light some key principles to apply to any pastoral transition, whatever the mechanics of finding a successor might be in a particular church. In these narratives, no actual names of churches or individuals are used, though the stories themselves are factual and show us how well—or sometimes how poorly—these transitions can go.

Practical Questions for Consideration

1. Investigate more fully some of the biblical narratives mentioned in this chapter. If the transitions went well, what contributed to them going well? If they went poorly, what contributed to them going poorly?

2. What current or potential parallels to the leadership transitions mentioned in this chapter do you see in your own congregation?

-3-

When the Transition
Goes Well

~~~

Northside Presbyterian Church

"I Hope He'll Be Here to Bury Me"

Bill Jeffers began his pastoral ministry at Northside Presbyterian Church (NPC) and served there for over thirty years, enjoying great popularity with his congregation throughout his ministry. Bill had a humble, unassuming personality; and he established special relationships with the people in his congregation through his own personal evangelism, ongoing interaction, and personal friendship. Most descriptions of Bill's strengths in ministry over the years were not so much what one would think of as ministerial gifts, but elements of his personal character. He was not a dynamic preacher or teacher, but his messages expressed his own spiritual maturity and wisdom, and were very helpful to those who heard him week after week. Over the years, his congregation grew to become one of the larger churches in the city.

Though the personal qualities Bill possessed caused him to be loved greatly by his congregation, he was seen as lacking in leadership and organizational ability. Some of this assessment may have been more perceived than actual, but some of it was accurate, according to some of his fellow elders. He tended to acquiesce to the desires of church members if they wanted to implement a new program or ministry, as long as they didn't go against any biblical principle.

Bill eventually desired to scale back his ministry activity and schedule and began to think toward stepping down from his pastoral position (though he would continue some teaching ministries he had developed over the years). He first discussed the need for a succession plan with one of his elders. He later met with a group of elders, who agreed that a step-by-step succession plan for the church was needed. These elders formed a confidential, ad hoc succession committee that met with Bill to formulate the plan. After a few months, this committee told the whole Session that it had been working with Bill on a timetable for the leadership transition. Thus, when Bill made the final decision to step down, the Session was ready to see the congregation through the transition.

The Session played the primary role in determining the demographics of the search committee. Once the demographics were established, the majority of the committee was elected by the congregation, with other members having been chosen by the Session and the Diaconate from their membership.

The Session also had determined beforehand that the search committee would report directly to the congregation, not to the Session. This was its understanding of the process set forth in the PCA's *Book of Church Order* (*BCO*). Richard, a search committee member, felt this method provided the committee an advantage as it went about its work. He said, "I think the process that we followed was much better than taking it to the Session. I've always felt like a small committee can dig in and get the information and debate it a whole lot better."

As it began to meet, the committee identified three key qualities needed by the successor pastor. First, the successor needed to be consistent with the theology of the PCA and have some specific ministry practices that the committee felt were needed. Second, he needed to be comfortable with Northside's specific ministry emphases. Third, the committee wanted someone who would have the personal qualities that would help him to follow a long-term popular pastor like Bill.

As they reflected on those personal qualities, the committee knew they would need someone with a strong enough personality to weather the challenges of succeeding Bill. As one committee member said, "You've got to find somebody that is strong. A weak person couldn't take it." Also, while the committee initially might have wanted to find a carbon copy of Bill, they also realized that wasn't really possible, and they ultimately wanted to find someone who was neither a carbon copy nor the exact opposite of Bill. The committee recognized that they hoped for someone who had some of the gifts that Bill lacked, specifically someone who had the strong organizational skills which Bill did not possess.

The committee completed its work in less than a year. Since Bill had agreed to remain at Northside until a new pastor was called, the committee sought to work through specific steps along a timeline which would end at the actual transition from Bill to the successor pastor. They sought possible candidates' names from the congregation and from Bill himself, since he was familiar with most of the ministers who might be candidates to succeed him. The committee eventually narrowed down the number of candidates to around ten, then to around five, after reviewing resumes, audio sermons, and visiting other churches to hear candidates preach.

A group of committee members also talked with Clyde Rollins, an experienced and well-respected pastor who was considerably younger than Bill. Initially, the committee did not approach him as a candidate, but as one who could counsel them regarding their pastoral search. He advised the committee not to call someone who would be intimidated by Bill, were he to continue ministering in the area. He said, "It's so important to keep Bill there, so we want somebody who loves Bill and admires Bill and would want Bill, not somebody who wants to get rid of Bill." After another team visited with Clyde, the committee as a whole ultimately came to the conclusion that it was in fact Clyde himself who was the best candidate to succeed Bill.

Clyde and his wife visited a worship service at Northside and met with the search committee. He had preached at Northside previously, so he was somewhat known to the congregation. After much prayer, he and his wife agreed to come to Northside should a call be issued. The search committee recommended him to the congregation, which voted to call him as their next pastor.

Clyde appeared to enjoy an initial, "honeymoon" period with the congregation. Harris, who served on the search committee, said that Clyde "was received initially great—people loved him." Attendance increased substantially during Clyde's first few months as pastor. His preaching style contrasted Bill's and this factor, coupled with his newness following a long-term pastor, contributed significantly to the increased attendance. Richard said, "People were just curious to hear the new preacher. It was exciting. His preaching style was so different. Bill was kind of quiet, calm, and very soft. Clyde is very energetic. He brought energy."

However, soon there were dissident groups that started to find fault with the new pastor as significant changes that Clyde initiated brought dissatisfaction with some members of the congregation. At Clyde's initiation the Session made changes in the church's worship service style and schedule, upsetting some members. He also sought to restructure the Session and Diaconate for more effective and efficient ministry, creating a perceived loss of personal control or power that displeased certain individual officers.

Dissatisfaction with Clyde also arose among some members because of his personality and how it impacted his preaching style. Clyde has a public persona that, according to the committee members, is misinterpreted and that led some people to dislike him. His style was much more loud and animated than Bill's, leading to the charge that he was not humble. This, according to Harris, is not correct: "Old Clyde is a 'blunder buster,' you know. He's strong and loud. Bill was quiet and sweet. I know Clyde Rollins and I know he's a humble man. He loves the Lord."

The *content* of Clyde's preaching differed from that of Bill also. Some persons are simply overwhelmed at the amount of information he provides in one sermon. Jane, a search committee member, said, somewhat tongue in cheek, that Bill "would have his three points and a poem. And Clyde would have his seventeen life-take-aways after having fourteen points. But that's overwhelming for some people. They would give anything to have three points and a poem." Eventually, many of the more dissatisfied members left the church for other congregations.

In addition, some church members were dissatisfied with Northside for things unrelated to Clyde (such as a lack of desired programs for certain age groups). Also, newer congregations in the area appealed to some people, leading them to depart from Northside as well. However, though there were significant numerical losses to the congregation, it gained at least as many members as it lost during Clyde's first few years.

Though Clyde met dissatisfaction both at the congregational and Sessional levels, for the most part he weathered the difficult times he faced. Harris summarized the situation, saying, "At first it was exciting—a new pastor! It was total acceptance, and then dissidents arose. But they've gone now and in my opinion everything is going well."

In the long run, the transition from Bill to Clyde has worked. A large part of the congregation is well satisfied with Clyde and his ministry. Almost one fourth of the congregation has joined since he came and clearly considers him to be "their" pastor. Though part of the congregation would like him to be different in particular areas of ministry, most hold their views in a way that is not contentious. Richard attributes the success of the transition to three primary factors: Bill's personal humility, particularly in his relationship with Clyde; Clyde's honoring of Bill; and the Session's steadfast support of Clyde, even amid opposition he faced on the part of some elders. Richard related a Session meeting at which one elder noted how the Israelites who had followed Moses' leadership also followed the leadership of his successor, Joshua—and urged the Northside elders to follow that same pattern with Bill and Clyde. For the most part, they have done so.

In regard to Bill's relationship with Clyde, both men have been strong enough—and humble enough—to be supportive of each other. Richard said, "If somebody came to Bill and complained about the way Clyde was doing something, Bill wouldn't listen to that. He would always defer to Clyde." Clyde also has sought to pay honor to Bill. Though he has instituted changes, he never prefaced those changes with "That's the way Bill did it, but we aren't going to do it that way anymore."

The members of the search committee felt that prayer played an important role amid their search process. While efforts in prayer were not highly organized, they nevertheless took place. Harris put it simply, saying, "We prayed and prayed and searched and searched and we got a man of God." Richard felt there was a connection between the prayers of the committee and the way different elements came together for Clyde to accept the call to Northside. The Lord's hand was evident throughout the process.

Richard referred to his participation on the committee as "an exhilarating experience, an interesting experience" which he would participate in again if needed. Jane echoed this sentiment saying, "I would do it again. I don't think I'll have the opportunity to do it again. I hope I don't. I hope Clyde will be here to bury me." The committee has a sense of satisfaction with the job that was done and a confidence that God superintended them in the various phases of their work.

Practical Questions for Consideration

1. How do you see your own congregation reflected in the circumstances or characters of this transition? Suggest three or four specifics that come to mind.

2. Which parties contributed to the success of this transition? What did they do specifically?

3. This transition ultimately went well—but what factors had to be overcome in the process in order for this to happen?

4. Were there things that could have been done by individuals or groups to make this an even smoother transition?

5. How can you apply the lessons of this transition to the specific context of your own congregation? List two or three ways the lessons of this transition apply to your situation.

– 4 –

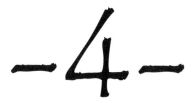

When Things Fall Apart

~~~

Forest Hills Presbyterian Church

"He Looked the Least Like John"

John Rutledge served as senior pastor of Forest Hills Presbyterian Church for sixteen years. He was a "people person" and was very approachable. His love and genuine concern for his congregation were obvious. Members of his congregation knew he was available if they ever wanted to call and talk with him about a situation in their lives. He spent many hours in prayer and often prayed with people immediately if they shared a problem. He was well loved by his congregation, particularly because of his willingness to be available to them. Many people joined the church over the years because of the personal connection and friendship they had with him. His personal warmth and genuine concern endeared him to people, and he was appreciated by all age groups. The congregation grew steadily in numbers over the years John was pastor, though the growth plateaued somewhat in the last two years of his tenure.

John was not a particularly strong preacher. While his preaching was biblically based, it tended to be somewhat repetitive from week to week. In addition, he was not a very good administrator, and he lacked organizational skills. Toward the end of his tenure, his Session as a whole perceived a lack of leadership in the hard areas where they needed someone to help them focus or someone to "referee" discussions between them. Several elders, because of their business background, were goal-oriented and felt the church should be run in a "businesslike" way. So, for all of his godliness and pastoral ministry, John did not provide the style of leadership they desired. Even his popularity may have been due in part to his discomfort with conflict. As one elder explained, "Sometimes if you don't take a stand for something, then you don't irritate other people. It would be hard for someone to say that they had a problem with John over an issue, because sometimes he would not take a stand on an issue. He didn't want to get in the middle of conflicts."

The tension between who John was as a person and pastor and what the Session desired became increasingly clear to John. He recognized that the Session wanted another type of pastor and believed God wanted him to serve elsewhere. After much prayer, he began to pursue another place of ministry and eventually decided to accept a call from another church.

His departure and the subsequent transition were not easy for the congregation. Because of the personal connection many members had with John, the church went through a grieving process after he left. One member felt the Session failed to address the issue of grief in a sensitive way. He said, "It was like, 'Well, he's been with us for a long time, he's gone, so goodbye.'"

After John had left, the Session called a congregational meeting at which a pastoral search committee was elected. The committee was quite diverse in its membership in terms of church background and theological views, reflecting the diversity that existed in the Forest Hills congregation at the time. For the most part the committee felt the Session provided little guidance for them even though the search committee members were inexperienced in conducting a pastoral search. According to Shirley, a search committee member, "It was the first time the church had been through anything like that. It was new to everybody. I don't think anyone on our committee had ever served on a search committee." She said that she and the other committee members were somewhat naïve as to the potential realities of a transition process under the circumstances they faced. She said, "We were a little blind about thinking about what a bad experience with a pastor could be, because we had not experienced that." The committee itself formulated a church profile related to things such as the emphasis the church placed on missions, the importance the church placed on financial giving, and the congregation's interests and demographics. The committee next began to build a pastoral profile, establishing the specific qualities desired in the next pastor.

The search committee considered what the church's elders seemed to want in a pastor, and this impacted the committee's profile. Ben, another committee member, said he thought leadership was looking for a way to get the church to grow. "They felt we had a lot of potential. The "kindling" was there—all we needed was a good spark to set the thing off. The elders were looking for someone dynamic." One quality John possessed that the committee *did* desire in the new pastor was experience in pastoral ministry. However, on the whole, the pastoral profile that developed was more of a reaction to John's personality and ministry. Most on the committee desired someone who would provide a significant contrast to the previous pastor. As Ben, explained, "We were tired of John's weaknesses, so therefore our priorities were the opposite of John."

After examining the résumés of a number of candidates, the committee's attention was drawn to Will Kessling. He had been recommended by a friend of the congregation and had submitted his résumé. Committee members listened to some of his sermons and met with him as a group. Eventually he also preached a few times at Forest Hills (as did other potential candidates), so others in the congregation also became familiar with him.

As they got to know him better, many on the committee were quite impressed with Will. Three particular things brought this about: his written résumé, his preaching, and his apparent leadership abilities. However, one thing Will did not have was pastoral experience. He was a relatively recent seminary graduate. Thus he lacked a key element the committee had set forth as part of its pastoral profile.

In regard to Will's preaching ability, he especially contrasted John's weakness in this area. Will's preaching style was much more dynamic and thought provoking than John's. Ben said, "You knew where he stood. When you got to the end of the sermon, you knew what he had said. He was a good preacher. We were thirsty people, and we rushed to the water." Most of all however, Will impressed the committee because, as Ben said, "He looked the least like John of all the candidates. I don't think that was ever said, but that is the bottom line. He looked the least like John."

At points along the way the committee felt a degree of pressure from different sources—especially the Session—to conclude the search process and recommend Will to the congregation. Shirley observed that "there were a few elders that were not on the committee that really wanted Will, that really liked his preaching style. They began to talk about it within the congregation and they approached us openly, saying they really thought he was the one, and asking what we were waiting on. It was very obvious and preferences were made known. I think that sped up the process."

Eventually Will was called as the congregation's pastor. He enjoyed a "honeymoon" period with his new congregation, with things generally going well for a few weeks after he began his ministry at Forest Hills. The congregation was excited about having a new pastor. They appreciated the fact that Will was able to connect people to various ministries in the church, even as his predecessor had done. They liked Will's preaching, and initially some people liked his stronger personality and more assertive leadership style when compared with his predecessor.

Yet, although the committee had looked to find a new pastor who was different from John, the congregation began to miss the very personal, pastoral ministry John had provided that Will did not. The congregation was grieving over the loss of their minister of many years and needed someone who would provide loving pastoring to the church. Some members felt Will simply did not provide this to any great degree. His lack of pastoral experience may have made him insensitive to this need. His emphasis appeared to be more on pushing his agenda for the church than on caring for the people of the congregation. While he had many personal interactions with people these tended to be very quick; to some members he came across as if he was checking them off his list in order to get to the next person rather than being concerned for them individually.

Will also implemented changes in a very forceful way. Ben said, "We had sixteen years of a preacher who never pushed anything"—providing another huge contrast to this new pastor. One leader described it as "the culture of intimidation—intimidation and hurry and 'it's my way or the highway.' From John's no leadership hardly at all, it was like a whiplash." Art said, "The idea of being rejected didn't set well with Will. If he had presented something and something hadn't gone exactly as he thought, it seemed to get to him."

People began to see Will as lacking humility—a stark contrast to his predecessor—and over time a great deal of friction developed between Will and his Session. While several Session members had wanted a "strong" leader who would contrast John's perceived lack of leadership ability, in the words of Ben, "They got more than they bargained for!" Problems inevitably developed between Will and the Session when its members differed with Will's proposals or ideas. Ron said, "They asked for a leader, they got a leader, and then there was his sense that they were not following him. He went about it with an 'either you're on my side, or you're against me' approach."

Hostilities also developed between Will and other staff members when his ideas met with disagreement. The hostility of these different relationships continued to escalate to the point where Will's motives often were questioned, particularly by the Session. Some elders who had been strongly in favor of calling Will as pastor eventually changed their opinion about him and desired that he be removed from his position. In Ben's view, they went on a "crusade" to have Will removed as pastor—an approach Ben did not agree with. Nevertheless, less than four years after Will's succeeding a long-term pastor, the elders agreed that the negatives of having him as pastor far outweighed the positives. He was asked by his Session to resign and did so, ending a tumultuous pastoral tenure. Thus, the congregation would need to begin a pastoral search once again.

Yet, the transition wasn't doomed to failure merely because Will followed a long-term pastor. One church member said that if the successor "had been a truly godly, humble man, I think he would probably still be here." Others echoed these sentiments, saying that if the successor had focused primarily on preaching and teaching and been less given to confrontation, the transition could have worked. However, Ben perhaps summed up things best: "We were looking for a 'non-John.' That was the main thing. And that led to our mistake."

Practical Questions for Consideration

1. How do you see your own congregation reflected in the circumstances or characters of this transition? Suggest three or four specifics that come to mind.

2. Do you agree with Ben's observation that looking for a pastor opposite the previous pastor was the primary error in this transition?

3. What other factors (if any) or dynamics contributed to the failure of the transition? What mistakes were made along the way?

4. Do you agree that this transition after a long-term pastor could have worked?

5. How could the Session have helped the transition go more smoothly? The search committee? The successor pastor?

6. How can you apply the lessons of this transition to the specific context of your own congregation? List two or three ways the lessons of this transition apply to your situation.

-5-

When Results Are Mixed

~~~

Immanuel Presbyterian Church

"We Know Whose Church It Is."

Glenn Mabry was the pastor of Immanuel Presbyterian Church (IPC) for over three decades, beginning his ministry there very early in the church's history. Glenn had a warm pastoral style and was able to develop relationships with the people already in the congregation. As the church expanded, Glenn taught the new member class which enabled him to continue to develop relationships with each member. He also taught the church's communicants' class, forming special bonds with the children of the church as they considered church membership. Thus, even as the congregation became larger, he was able to have a personal connection with the entire church body. The church's membership expanded steadily over his tenure and new facilities were constructed. Glenn was also a gifted teacher and was able to present scriptural truth in a way that his congregation enjoyed.

Brian, an elder in church, who also served on the search committee that found Glenn's successor, said, "Glenn was sort of everybody's father or big brother. He was dearly, dearly loved by the congregation. I believe he knew every member by name. That sounds impossible, but I rarely saw him miss somebody's name." Ken, also an elder, echoed this sentiment by describing Glenn's relationship with the congregation as one of "warmth and closeness. He had a pastoral style. Glenn was a much loved person."

Despite his wonderful skills as a preacher and pastor, Glenn wasn't gifted with great administrative or leadership skills—and neither was his Session. One elder noted, "There was not a strong leadership within the church. We did not have a strong Session."

Eventually Glenn was approached by a Christian organization and asked to consider becoming the organization's director. Glenn gradually told people that he was considering a new place of ministry; after first informing a small group of elders, he eventually informed the entire Session, and then the entire congregation. They prayed with him as he considered the new calling. In time, he did step down as pastor of IPC in order to accept the new position. A search committee was formed and began its work.

The search and transition were not easy. As one committee member said, "We had no idea what to do! We knew we had to do something, but what were we going to do? We were starting all over from scratch and we had to try to explain to the congregation what a search committee was." While the church had searched for associate pastors and other personnel in the past, the process of seeking a senior pastor was much more momentous.

Once the committee did begin to function, the members had conflicting ideas about what the direction of the church should be. One committee member explained, "Glenn had been at our church for thirty years and the church was what it was. No one had challenged that, then suddenly there was a vacuum because he left. People rushed into the vacuum and began pursuing their own agendas as they tried to take the church in a direction that it had not gone before. There was conflict within the search committee about what the desired direction should be. The chairman of the committee explained, "I think a majority of the committee wanted . . . not somebody who was going to quickly whittle us down to 120 'true believers.' . . . There were some people that really wanted to move us way in that direction. . . . But they were the same folks that also made it a bloody mess once Tom (the new minister) got here. They had wanted us to go some place and we didn't go there."

The congregation clearly went through a process of grieving when Glenn left, and, to some extent, it continues even to this day. Ken said that Immanuel saw "all the classic symptoms of the grieving process. People get loyal to the man. They (pastors) are loved and now they are gone." One older widow in the church said—even after Glenn's successor had arrived— "First I lose my husband and then I lose my pastor." Her grief was very real.

After a year and a half of searching, the committee recommended Tom Evans, an experienced PCA pastor. The congregation agreed and he came to Immanuel and has now been there for over eight years. When Tom arrived, he initially was received warmly by most members of the Session and the congregation but also with the mindset that "you've got big shoes to fill." Others were less kind to him. Among the issues that caused some people not to receive Tom well initially was the fact that he did not know who they were. Nolan said, "There was a group of folks who were offended that he didn't remember who they were. Tom had just met them once along with fifty other people. They were sad cases." Tom also faced a degree of difficulty relating to some of the members of the congregation because he was from a different region of the country—some of the things he talked about were fixtures in the culture in which he was raised, but they were somewhat foreign to his new congregation.

However, the greatest initial problem area for Tom in relation to the congregation came in the area of preaching. Some felt he was not theologically sound or not "Reformed" enough (though most elders dispute this). Others believed he was not "relaxed" enough in the pulpit—that he was too dependent on his notes. Some didn't like the fact that he didn't go through a passage verse by verse, as Glenn had done (though Tom's messages were still focused well on the scriptural passage at hand).

Brian said, "There was this element that made his life very unpleasant. As a result, his preaching was not as good as it had been previously because he was nervous. You know, how you would feel if there was somebody up there writing down every word? Tom would find himself making statements just to prove he was Reformed."

In reality, the biggest difficulty Tom *actually* faced early on in his tenure at Immanuel was the simple fact that he was following Glenn, who had served as a long-term pastor. While some members of the congregation may not have agreed with Glenn on particular issues, no one was willing to mount any real challenge, due to his long tenure. Brian said, "People had either decided they were going to live with the way Glenn was or they had left. So even people who didn't agree with Glenn had this warm relationship with Glenn and loved him and they weren't going to challenge him. They were not going to try to move the church. When somebody new came in, they were ready to challenge because the new guy has no inherent power."

As a result, Tom endured a period of opposition that lasted approximately two years. This was the length of time it took until several elders rotated on to the Session who were closer to Tom's theology and ministry philosophy and thus able to support him via the church's governing body. Ultimately, most of the individuals who were accusatory in their relationship with Tom have since left the congregation. They were not able to gain a sufficient power base to accomplish their desire of having the church go in a particular direction or have Tom preach in the way they desired.

The transition resulted in a significant measure of attrition among the church's membership. There were three "waves of exodus" of people from the congregation that occurred following the transition from Glenn to Tom. First to leave were people who, as Brian said, "had other agendas; they needed to leave; that was okay." A second wave of people with less specific reasons for leaving then departed over a period of several months. Then, a third wave of people left, with the biggest common factor being that they didn't like Tom's preaching.

While Tom was not able to know as many people immediately as Glenn had known at the end of his tenure, he has relational skills similar to those Glenn possessed. He carries on conversations with people in the hallways after worship, and he and his wife entertain church members in their home. He has been able to get to know many people in the church and continues to form relationships with new members just as Glenn did.

The search committee had desired a relationship between the former and successor pastors in which the new pastor would not have a problem with the previous pastor returning to the church for special occasions in the life of the congregation. This relationship came to fruition. Tom and Glenn developed very quickly a warm and cordial relationship that continues this day. Tom asked Glenn to preach at the service at which Tom was installed as Immanuel's pastor—something Glenn was very willing to do. In addition, at different times Tom sought Glenn's counsel and Glenn was willing to provide it. They treasure each other's friendship.

Tom withstood the initial, very personal attacks upon

him. He has done so, in the words of Ken, with "humility and total reliance on God's strength." He appears to have solid support from his Session and from most of the congregation. Today he also plays a major role of leadership in his Presbytery, as does the IPC congregation itself.

It seems that the transition has had mixed results—there were major difficulties in Tom's early years, but things have settled down. Ken believes that the mantle of leadership is now firmly in Tom's hands. He said, "For many years it was 'Glenn's' church. Now after almost eight years I think it's 'Tom's' church—though we know whose church it really is."

Practical Questions for Consideration

1. How do you see your own congregation reflected in the circumstances or characters of this transition? Suggest three or four specifics that come to mind.

2. How did the fact that the predecessor pastor had served this church for so many years contribute to the difficulty of the transition?

3. Could any of the struggles that were part of this transition have been avoided? How?

4. In this transition, what role did grief play in a negative reaction to a new pastor?

5. What role did the Session of Immanuel Church play in helping this transition end up better than it could have? What roles did the predecessor and successor pastor play?

6. How can you apply the lessons of this transition to the specific context of your own congregation? List two or three ways the lessons of this transition apply to your situation.

– 6 –

What Makes These Transitions Go Poorly?

What can cause transitions after a long-term pastor to go poorly? For one thing, the process is often unknown. When a long-term pastor leaves, a church will not have searched for a new pastor for a considerable length of time. It's quite possible that no one in the congregation will have served on a search committee before. If a pastoral tenure spans over multiple decades, very few people in the church will have any experience in how to go about the transition. And, when the transitions do occur, a number of factors can cause them to be problematic.

"Now's Our Chance"

Searches and transitions can suffer when they are used by individuals or groups in a congregation to seize an opportunity to change the direction of the church. This was clearly seen at Immanuel. Brian mentioned the "vacuum" that existed after Glenn's departure—which several people sought to fill with a new agenda and direction for the church that were contrary to those that existed during long-term pastor Glenn's tenure. They saw potential for affecting a theological and practical shift in the church. Ultimately they were unsuccessful, but their efforts created great challenges for the search committee, the Session, and the successor pastor.

Similarly, some members of the Session of Forest Hills saw the opportunity to have the type of pastor they had desired for some time—a strong leader who would guide the church with skills which long-term pastor John had lacked. While a desire to meet the pastoral needs of a congregation is good, in this case people quickly went after what they *wanted* rather than accurately and patiently assessing what the congregation *needed*.

"We Need Help!"

Another factor that plays a role in the success or failure of a transition is the leadership role of the Session in the process. There's a delicate balance that must be struck when it comes to Sessional involvement with search committees. On the one hand, once a committee has begun its work, its members need to be free to do that work without interference and pressure from Session members. On the other hand, Sessions should provide guidance to search committees as they begin their work. The work of search committees would be more efficient if Sessions would formulate the pastoral profile before committees begin their searches. Search committees then could *begin* with their actual searches and pursue candidates who fit within the general parameters of the profile established by the Session. This practice also retains the Session in the primary leadership role in the congregation.

The same practice of sessional leadership should follow in regard to a congregational profile. Normally a congregational profile should not be used to determine the future philosophical direction of a church's ministry. Rather, it should be used to clarify or reflect the existing ministry bent. If for some reason this tool *is* used to determine a new direction in ministry philosophy, this is the responsibility of the Session, not a pastoral search committee.

A lack of sessional guidance can leave search committees feeling somewhat helpless. This happened at Forest Hills, where Shirley felt the Session should have been involved in developing the pastoral profile. Then, the committee could have sought a pastor who matched the profile as closely as possible. Instead, she said the development of the profile "was all the committee," which had a "huge diversity" as they sought to determine the right type of pastor the congregation needed.

The Session can help the committee begin its search more quickly when profiles are already in place. In addition, having the profiles in place for the committee helps it to know the type pastor to search for—*and* the type congregation the new pastor will be serving.

"We Feel Rushed!"

Search committees sometimes become frustrated because of a real or perceived expectation that they are not moving fast enough. Sessions as well as congregations can serve search committees well by supporting them during the search process and allowing them to do what they have been charged to do, even if it takes what seems to be a long time. The transition at Forest Hills suffered because the process was unnecessarily rushed. The Forest Hills Session interfered with the work of the pastoral search committee by pushing its members to go ahead and recommend a particular candidate. It placed a great amount of unnecessary pressure on the committee to reach a decision before some members were ready to do so.

Also, committees themselves need realism in terms of the time it is taking them to decide on the right successor. Ben, for example, said he felt the Forest Hills committee had been through a "marathon-type" search and was "tired of the whole thing" when they recommended Will. In reality, the committee had only been at work about half a year. It may have been a hard, busy, pressure-filled time, but searches often take longer. The belief that the Forest Hills committee had been through a "marathon" search showed an unrealistic view of the search process—a view perhaps shared both by members of the Session as they rushed the committee, and by members of the committee who wanted to be done with their search. Sessions can also encourage and pray with committees if committee members begin to become frustrated amid their search.

Looking for Mr. Opposite—Or Mr. Clone

Another factor that impacts pastoral searches negatively is basing the search for a new pastor on who the predecessor has been. It's possible to seek a successor who is just the opposite—or just like—his predecessor—and both are mistakes. One of the greatest errors made by the majority of the Forest Hills search committee was seeking someone who was opposite their former pastor in several personal and ministry areas. They found that person, and the transition failed miserably. On the whole, the Session of Forest Hills seemed to have little understanding of the impact of a long-term pastor on a congregation. Their desire for someone opposite pastor John showed a lack of awareness of the congregation's need for someone who could "connect" with them as John had done. Both the Session and the search committee failed to take into account the impact of the difference in the personalities of their former and successor pastors. Both groups suffered greatly from a reaction to some of the weaknesses of the departing long-term pastor. As Will said, "We were looking for a 'non-John.'" They clearly sought a person with opposite characteristics from their previous pastor—and they achieved this, to the detriment of the pastoral transition and the life of the congregation.

On the other hand, to seek an exact copy of the previous pastor would be a mistake for a search committee as well. Such a man does not exist, and to pursue him would be fruitless and would keep the congregation focused on the past instead of moving toward the future. The committee at Northside recognized that there was no "carbon copy" of Bill Jeffers. The committee didn't want a "clone" of Bill, but someone with a little different package of characteristics. They sought and found someone who could fit within the ministry philosophy of Northside.

The successor pastor should possess the ministry strengths of the predecessor which have helped define the ministerial character and philosophy of the congregation. It's true that a congregation may indeed benefit from a new pastor who possesses ministerial gifts which the long-term pastor did not have. This occurred both at Northside and at Immanuel. However, if there are areas in which he appears to have gifts the long-term pastor did not possess (such as leadership or organization, for example), the committee should investigate whether he exercises those gifts in humility, in submission to his fellow elders, and in pursuit of the edification of the body of Christ.

Practical Questions for Consideration

1. Suppose your pastor were to announce tomorrow that he plans to step down in a few weeks. What segments of your congregation might see this as their opportunity to change the direction or identity of the church—either theologically or in terms of ministry practices?

2. How can your church's leadership respond well to attempts to change the direction or identity of the church, if the people involved in these efforts are not among the church's elected leadership?

3. What will the potential fallout be if leadership responds to these efforts? If it doesn't respond?

4. In your congregation's unique circumstances, what are specific ways church leadership could serve a search committee without interfering in the committee's work?

-7-

What Can Help These Transitions Go Well?

Transitions after a long-term pastor really can go well! Though they are difficult, they aren't necessarily doomed to failure. Conventional wisdom may affirm that the successor to a long-term pastor is inevitably a "sacrificial lamb" destined to have a short tenure, but this doesn't have to be the case. In the Immanuel and Northside congregations this phenomenon didn't occur, even though both successors followed beloved predecessors. While certainly each successor endured his own set of problematic issues, both cases show that the ultimate results of these transitions can be quite positive.

There are several individuals and groups involved in the process of a transition after a long-term pastor, and each can play a part in facilitating a healthy transition. Let's think through how the different parties can help make the transition work.

Departing Pastors

The long-term pastor can enhance the transition process both before and after he departs his congregation. Before he leaves, he can benefit his church by helping it prepare adequately for his departure. This should involve leading his Session to develop a transition or succession plan (see Appendix A). At Forest Hills Presbyterian Church, where the transition went very poorly, no transition plan was in place, and apparently nothing regarding the transition had been thought out by the Session. In the congregations where the transitions went well or had even mixed results, some careful succession planning had taken place. If the pastor has led his elders to prepare a transition plan, it will be in place at that inevitable time he is led of God to move from his current congregation. The Session then can proceed in a more orderly manner into the process of pastoral transition. While they may be inexperienced in seeking a pastor, they will have help available because they have been prepared for the process.

The departing pastor also can help prepare his whole *congregation* for the process that awaits them. Through personal interaction and writing, he should remind the congregation that it faces a search process that may be lengthy and that needs to be approached prayerfully. He should urge members to embrace his successor in love, with prayer, and without a critical spirit. In doing so, he's equipping the congregation to move beyond mere change to genuine transition.

Then once he leaves, the departing pastor must be willing to humbly accept the congregation's actually doing what he has encouraged it to do in terms of welcoming and supporting the new pastor. Rather than being threatened by the love that is shown to the successor pastor, he should rejoice in that pastor's ministry successes. Glenn Mabry at Immanuel provided an excellent model of how a departing pastor should respond to the congregation having a new shepherd. His willingness to preach at Tom's installation service demonstrated that he could relinquish the mantle of leadership to Tom. He served as a colleague in ministry rather than a competitor and provided a quality example to his former church.

Finally, the long-term pastor has a responsibility to truly *leave* his congregation. While he will maintain friendships with members of his congregation, it is vital that he allow the church to function without any interference from him, and that he recognize his new role as a *former* pastor.

Sessions

Sessions can help the transition process both by the under-standing they provide their congregations and by the more formal, practical responsibilities they carry out. They first need an appreciation of the sense of loss and grief congrega-tions experience when a long-term pastor leaves. In each church we've looked at, there was an attachment to the depart-ing pastor and a difficulty in "letting go" when he left. Just as we should not expect someone to quickly "move on" following the death of a close family member, elders should not expect members of their congregations to quickly "move on" follow-ing the departure of one to whom they have had a very close spiritual relationship for many years. Brian related the story of an older woman at Northside who compared the loss of her pastor to the death of her own husband. It was so difficult for her to deal with that she chose not to attend worship services. Some members will have deeper and longer experiences of grief than others. Nevertheless, grief is an emotion which Ses-sions should expect their members to exhibit when their long-term pastor leaves.

Art, an elder and search committee member at Forest Hills, felt that many in the church went through a definite grieving process upon John's departure. He also believed the Session failed to minister adequately to those who were grieving. He felt the Session could have helped by meeting with the congre-gation informally. In such a setting, the Session could have addressed where the congregation was in its corporate life, allowed people in the congregation to voice the sadness they felt, and had a time of prayer with the congregation. He said the "Session's making it known that we were still a church and we loved one another and that we were available for whatever the congregation needed" would have been beneficial in dealing with the grieving process.

When responsible Sessions come to terms with the grief their congregations are facing, they will be less prone to urge search committees to secure a pastor who is a stark contrast to the long-term pastor. The Forest Hills Session violated this principle, to the detriment of the pastoral transition. Also, as they understand the grief process congregations are facing, Sessions acting with wisdom will not rush search committees into a quick recommendation. Following a long-tenured pastor, the congregation needs some time to grieve. Going through the grief process gets congregations ready to embrace the next pastor. And, an extended period of vacancy may be just what a church needs to prepare emotionally for its new pastor.

As elders seek to assist with the grief process and to facilitate the psychological process of "letting go" during the time of pastoral transition, there are some practical steps they can take. One is to allow members to acknowledge what they feel at this point in their lives. This can be facilitated through a venue such as informal, small group meetings together with elders.

Another helpful step for Sessions is to involve the congregation in the transition process as early as possible through prayer. The congregation at Immanuel was brought into the process when it was asked to pray for Glenn Mabry as he considered a new ministry position. Not every situation can be discussed with the congregation as openly as this one was. However, when the congregation is involved in praying for the departing pastor at any point in the transition process, it is taken from a position as an outsider and moved into the process. Members also need to be involved in praying for the search committee throughout its work.

One goal of these practical steps is to bring about an inward, psychological embracing of the new pastor when he is found. Also, they give the membership a sense of ownership in the process, even though not every person is involved in the active search.

Sessions also need to decide whether it would be in the best interests of the congregation to call an interim pastor for at least some portion of the time in which their pastoral position is vacant. An interim pastor can provide a number of benefits. First, his presence helps alleviate the burden of additional responsibilities which otherwise would be placed on church officers during the time the congregation is without a regular pastor. In addition, in a congregation with additional pastoral staff, those staff members can continue to focus on the specific responsibilities for which they were called to the church, rather than assuming the duties normally filled by a lead pastor. Perhaps most importantly, when interim pastors are intentional in their ministry—not just filling the pulpit, but helping to shepherd a congregation through a transition and perhaps a difficult season of ministry—the interim pastor can serve as a bridge between the departing and successor pastors and help the congregation prepare for its next season of ministry.

An additional responsibility of the Session is to stand with the successor pastor against unjust opposition, such as that faced by Pastor Tom Evans at Immanuel Presbyterian Church. Elders should anticipate that some individuals or groups within the church may seek to advance personal agendas when the long-term pastor leaves. As in the case at Immanuel, some may pursue opportunities to grasp power within the church and need to be confronted and stopped as early as possible. Elders must be willing to resist mean-spirited attacks and the pursuit of personal agendas. They don't have to agree with the new pastor on every issue or promise their agreement with him on every idea or goal he has for the church. Yet, they should be willing to come to his defense against spiritual misconduct and take appropriate action, including the exercise of church discipline if it is warranted.

Pastoral Search Committees

The pastoral search committee receives much of the attention in the pastoral transition process. It will get much of the credit if the transition goes well and much of the blame if it doesn't. It bears tremendous responsibility to conduct its search carefully. The care it takes should be reflected in its evaluation of pastoral candidates and in patient and prayerful dependence upon the Lord as it goes about its work.

The primary mistake made by the majority of the Forest Hills search committee was seeking a successor pastor who was the opposite of his predecessor. They found that person, and the transition failed miserably. What they didn't realize was that the successor pastor was lacking in several of the areas in which their long-term pastor was gifted. Dr. Phil Douglass refers to this phenomenon as the "eighty-twenty rule" — referring to the gift mix of pastors. Churches sometimes find a successor pastor who has the twenty percent of an ideal gift mix the previous pastor *lacked* — while ignoring the fact that the successor doesn't have the eighty percent of gifts the departing pastor *did* have. The transition fails because the congregation doesn't need such a stark contrast in ministers.[20]

At Immanuel Presbyterian Church and Northside Presbyterian Church, the successors were different from their predecessors. Yet, each man also had ministry emphases similar to those of the long-term pastor, and each was able to operate within the ministry philosophy and emphases that drove his church. As a result, the effectiveness of the transition was enhanced greatly.

At the same time, the successor of a long-term pastor need not be an exact copy of his predecessor. An exact copy of the previous pastor doesn't exist and to pursue him is not only fruitless, but keeps the congregation focused on the past instead of moving toward the future. However, the successor pastor does need to possess the ministry strengths of the predecessor which have helped define the ministerial character and approach of the congregation. Members of the Northside committee recognized that there was no "carbon copy" of Bill Jeffers, and also that they didn't want a "clone" of Bill. They wisely sought someone who had a somewhat different package of characteristics, but who could still fit within the ministry philosophy of Northside.

A congregation *can* benefit from a new pastor who possesses ministerial gifts which the long-term pastor did not have. However, if there are areas in which he appears to have gifts which the long-term pastor did not possess, the committee should investigate whether he exercises those gifts in humility, in submission to his fellow elders, and in pursuit of the edification of the body of Christ.

Search committees also need to prayerfully seek God's provision of patience. This quality was lacking on the part of some members of the Forest Hills committee. They allowed the pressure they felt to build a sense of "hurry" into their search process, and it ended sooner than some committee members desired.

While it's entirely possible that the search process will be finished relatively quickly and the right man will be called to replace the long-term pastor, it's also quite possible that the process will take a considerable length of time. The failure to quickly locate a candidate to recommend is not an indication that the committee is failing to do its job. As Ken, an elder at Immanuel Presbyterian Church, pointed out, an "extended period of vacancy is the Lord's gift." The committee doesn't need to fear that extended period but should recognize its benefit if the Lord provides it. As the committee patiently and faithfully does its work, it can find the man of God's choosing whom it can recommend with confidence to succeed the long-term pastor.

Successor Pastors

Someone who follows a long-term pastor has a difficult job. Not only is pastoral ministry hard already, but the new minister is succeeding someone who very likely was appreciated by his congregation and provided them with a sense of security and comfort. They've become very used to him, even if they've recognized he isn't perfect. So, both the way the new pastor relates to his predecessor and the spirit he demonstrates in his ministry are vital to helping the transition go as well as possible.

Two key tenets a new pastor needs to keep in mind for a successful transition are: "Honor thy predecessor," and "Walk humbly." At Northside and Immanuel, the successor was neither intimidated by the church's memory of the predecessor nor by his ongoing relationship to the congregation. This helped smooth the transition from a long-term pastor. A humble willingness to honor one's predecessor, as was shown by these men, will help to provide a pastor a good beginning in his new place of ministry. When a successor demonstrates godly character, he's able to build up "relational capital" with his church's members and potentially attain a degree of longevity in the congregation.

In his leadership role, the new pastor should seek to lead his Session and congregation beyond mere change to genuine heart transition. He doesn't have to do things as they have always been done—in fact, he probably needs to implement some changes. However, he needs to convey the scriptural rationale for doing things in a different way. If a change can be explained to his elders, and if they are then given time to reflect upon it, there is a greater possibility they will internalize and accept it. The goal should be to lead them to transition rather than simply forcing them to change.

In addition, just plain perseverance is important for the new pastor. Tom Evans provided an example of this when he withstood the personal attacks that came upon him early in his tenure at Immanuel. The results of that perseverance were quite positive, as he now enjoys a stable ministry situation. The successor pastor can expect people to leave the congregation at different points after his arrival—it just goes with the territory in pastoral transitions. However, if he is willing to faithfully carry out the duties God has assigned him, he can expect to solidify his bond with the members of his congregation who remain. This bonding will occur as he ministers to them and grows in his relationships with them. He also can expect new members to come to the congregation who have an appreciation for the distinctives of his ministry.

Congregations
In a transition, especially after a long-term pastor, congrega-

tions need to give themselves permission to grieve. Each congregation whose experience of transition we've studied dealt with some degree of grief when their long-term pastor left. The attachment of members to a former pastor can become problematic if he becomes an idol to them or if they refuse to recognize the legitimate position of the new pastor. However, the mere presence of grief isn't harmful and can be part of a healthy transition process. In addition, just as we are to *grieve in hope* when a believer dies (1 Thessalonians 4:13), Christians amid a pastoral transition can grieve in hope because Christ is sufficient for the church He loves.

While grief is a reality in transitions, patience, on the other hand, doesn't come naturally—so congregations need to seek it prayerfully. A congregation can serve its search committee by waiting patiently for them to complete their work rather than rushing them. Some persons on the Forest Hills committee were pressured by church members to come to a decision and specifically to recommend Will Kessling. This hurried process contributed to a poor transition. As the congregation exercises patience in relation to the search committee, there is a much stronger probability that the committee will come to a recommendation with which the congregation is satisfied. Quality of the new pastor rather than speed of the search process should be the desire of the church.

Once the new pastor arrives, a congregation should examine itself to see if it is being realistic in its expectations. For example, the new pastor should not be expected to know his members' names when he begins his ministry (as was the expectation of some at Immanuel). In addition, the congregation should accept that the new pastor will be different from the former pastor in his temperament, in his mix of spiritual gifts, and in his ministry emphases. This will be a benefit in some cases and a detriment in others. If members will allow him to be who God has constituted and gifted him to be, give him an opportunity to minister and also seek to minister to him and with him, it's quite possible that *his* ministry will be one of long duration.

Practical Questions for Consideration

1. Does your church have a pastoral transition plan in place?

2. What specific elements do you believe should be included in a transition plan for your particular congregation?

3. What personal characteristics and ministry strengths is it *essential* for your next pastor to possess that are similar to those possessed by your current pastor?

4. What personal characteristics and ministry strengths would it be *desirable* for your next pastor to possess?

5. How could an interim pastor help serve as a bridge between your long-term pastor and his successor? If your congregation is in the midst of a transition after a long-term pastor, what are some specific benefits an interim pastor could bring to the church, given the unique dynamics of this transition?

-8-

Applying Biblical Principles to Transitions after a Long-Term Pastor

Pastors come and go—sometimes rather frequently and sometimes after a long stay. But ultimately all pastors leave their congregations. One thing that doesn't change, however, is the Lord's commitment to His church and His presence with His people. So, as we think of God's care and love for His church amid ministry transitions, there are principles we need to keep in mind.

First, He's graciously sovereign over all things. Ephesians 1:11 says that God "works all things according to the counsel of his will," while Romans 8:28 says that "for those who love God all things work together for good, for those who are called according to his purpose." Pastoral transitions that work out well *and* those that don't all occur under Jesus' gracious purpose and government. As Ken said about Immanuel church, "We know whose church it is." The church belongs to Christ, and even a poor transition, with the many difficulties it may bring, isn't random and can be utilized by the Lord for the good of His people and for His glory. So, God's people can *trust Him.*

Second, Jesus provides spiritual growth through the trial of our faith. Faith is tried amid waiting, amid trusting God's timing when a search committee doesn't seem to be in a big enough hurry, or when the new pastor just doesn't do everything like we wish he would. Yet when faith is tried, Jesus brings spiritual growth and maturity, teaches us more of Himself and the gospel, and teaches us to love people that may be hard to love—even as *He* faithfully loves those who are opposite spiritually to Himself. So, God's people can *focus on Him.*

Third, God will provide appropriate human instruments for His church at particular times. 1 Corinthians 3:5—7 says "What then is Apollos? What is Paul? Servants through whom you believed, as the Lord assigned to each. I planted, Apollos watered, but God gave the growth. So neither he who plants nor he who waters is anything, but only God who gives the growth." Paul was the one God provided to be the Corinthian church's spiritual father. Later, the church needed someone to keep things going, and God provided Apollos, who built on what Paul had done. They weren't exactly alike, nor were they opposites. Rather, God provided particular leaders and He utilized them at different stages in the life of the church. Each man, in each role, was important in God's plan, and each was dependent upon God's blessing for effectiveness. The church continued on as God graciously provided for its needs. God gives appropriate abilities and ministries to His church at particular seasons. He orders things for the blessing of His people. So, God's people can *rest in Him*.

Pastoral transitions are a process, and there will be phases within any of them that are easier or harder. It isn't just the end result of the process that determines how successful the transition really is, but also how its phases are perceived and handled along the way. So, these biblical principles, rooted in God's love and care for His church, need to be applied throughout the process.

These types of transitions are difficult. They *can* go well, but they won't go perfectly. The successor pastor inevitably will face opposition, possibly from among his fellow leaders, and most certainly from the congregation at large. A church will likely lose members. Those losses are not *necessarily* the fault of the successor pastor but they will occur, and he may be the one blamed.

However, it's also very possible that the congregation will gain new members under the leadership of the successor pastor—people who might not have joined under his predecessor. The successor can lead the church in fresh directions for ministry and can work toward developing his relationships with the long-time members of the church and solidify his position as *their* pastor.

Initial difficulties for the new pastor do not mean that the transition process has been a failure. Though the transition at Northside Presbyterian Church went generally well, Clyde Rollins still faced opposition fairly early in his ministry as he led specific changes in the congregation. However, today he continues to have a solid base of support among his officers and congregation. At Immanuel Presbyterian Church, Tom Evans endured more protracted and more overt opposition initially, yet ultimately things settled down and he had a stable situation. The opposition he faced was not an indication that the transition had failed.

The churches we looked at demonstrate the challenge of pastoral transitions after a long-term pastor. However, they also show that these transitions *can* work and that the difficulties of the process are not insurmountable. God can build His church and bring spiritual health and vitality to those congregations who are faced with replacing a pastor after many years of ministry. Through His grace He can facilitate a successful transition process when the long-term pastor leaves the local church.

Practical Questions for Consideration

1. In regard to God's purposes for your church, why is the process of pastoral transition just as important as the end result of the transition?

2. Has your church been through a transition after a long-term pastor? What specific truths of Scripture did God confirm to you during the process? How can you specifically apply these past lessons to future transitions?

3. How can you apply the biblical principles cited in this chapter to your prayers for the pastoral transition your church is facing or will face in the future?

Appendix A

~~~

Sample Transition Plan

Sample Transition Plan

1. Designation within the Session of a group which the pastor will inform when he is considering another ministry position or contemplating resigning or retiring

2. Commitment on the part of the smaller group and at some later point, on the part of the entire Session, to pray with the pastor regarding a different place of ministry, resignation, or retirement

3. A timetable for communicating the pastor's plans to the congregation should he decide to step down

4. A timetable for the pastor's departure

5. Determination by the Session if it desires to pursue an interim pastor

6. Determination of responsibilities for pulpit supply during the pastoral vacancy

7. Determination regarding restrictions on the departing pastor's ministry with the congregation once he leaves and determination as to whether these decisions will be left up to the successor pastor or whether the Session will set policies ahead of time

8. Development of pastoral and congregational profiles by the Session

9. Designation of the size of the pastoral search committee and its categories for membership (elders, deacons, women in the

church, congregation at large, etc.)

10. Establishment of how the search committee will report its recommendation

11. Election of the search committee by the congregation

12. Scheduling of an informal meeting to update the congregation on where the church is in its life, to allow the congregation to express any grief it may feel at the loss of its pastor, and to pray

13. Scheduling of ongoing updates of the congregation from the pastoral search committee

14. Scheduling of regular times for prayer for the church, the Session, and the pastoral search committee during the pastoral vacancy

Appendix B
~~~
# Checklists
# Before and During
# Transitions

# Points for Departing Pastors

1. Lead Session in developing a pastoral transition plan (see Appendix A).

2. Notify small group of elders when contemplating resigning or retiring.

3. Notify entire Session when contemplating resigning or retiring.

4. Communicate to Session the intention to step down.

5. Prepare congregation for departure through: personal interaction, writing, sermons.

# Points for Sessions

1.  Develop a pastoral transition plan (see Appendix A).

2.  Be alert to signs of grief or loss on the part of the congregation.

3.  Schedule congregational or small group meetings with elders to allow members to acknowledge feelings as the pastor departs.

4.  Develop a church profile (for use by search committee).

5.  Develop a pastoral profile (for use by search committee).

6.  Schedule times of prayer with congregation for transition process and pastoral search.

7.  Schedule updates from search committee to congregation.

# Points for Successor Pastors

1. Honor your predecessor in attitude and words.

2. Seek to build "relational capital" with your new congregation.

3. Where change is needed, convey the scriptural rationale for it to your fellow leaders.

4. Focus on godly character and leading with humility.

5. Seek to lead genuine heart transition in your church's ministry rather than merely forcing change.

6. Expect some attrition to occur, but build a bond with remaining congregants through faithful ministry to them.

7. Persevere in ministry.

# Points for Congregations

1. Don't be surprised by attrition amid the pastoral transition in your church.

2. Pray consistently and specifically for your new pastor and his family as they transition to their new place of ministry.

3. Purpose to minister in a personal way to your new pastor and his family and to join with him in the ministry of your congregation.

4. Pray for spiritual protection of your new pastor.

5. Pray that God would guard your new pastor from unrealistic expectations that could be placed upon him by others.

6. Ask yourself: Are my expectations of my new pastor realistic?

7. Give your new pastor the freedom be who God has constituted and gifted him to be.

# Appendix C

~~~

Ten Things Churches Need to Consider During Pastoral Transitions

(1) There Are Helpful, Biblical Examples of Transition

While the Bible doesn't set forth a fully developed theology of ministerial transition, it does provide several examples in which one spiritual leader succeeded another. In some cases, the previous leader had served for many years. These transitions resulted in different outcomes, with the succeeding leader attaining varying levels of success and acceptance by God's people. Study of the Old and New Testament passages related to transition helps remind us of God's interest in ministry transitions and can help us learn how to navigate them and what to expect when they come.

(2) Departing Pastors: Prepare Your Congregation

The departing pastor can enhance the transition process and demonstrate care for his congregation before he leaves by helping them prepare adequately for his departure. This should involve leading his Session to develop a transition or succession plan and have it in place well before he is even considering leaving. Then, when the whole congregation becomes aware he is leaving, he can help prepare them for the impending process that awaits them. Through personal interaction and writing, he should remind the congregation that it faces a search process that may be lengthy and that needs to be approached prayerfully. He should urge members to embrace his successor in love, with prayer, and without a critical spirit. In doing so, he's equipping the congregation to move beyond mere change to genuine transition. Every pastor will depart at some point. Help your church be as prepared as possible for that inevitable day.

(3) Expect To Grieve

Congregations need to give themselves permission to grieve when their pastor leaves. The attachment of members to a former pastor can become problematic if he becomes an idol to them or if they refuse to recognize the legitimate position of the new pastor. However, the mere presence of grief isn't harmful and can be part of a healthy transition process. Just as we are to *grieve in hope* when a believer dies (1 Thessalonians 4:13), Christians amid pastoral transitions can grieve in hope because Christ is sufficient for the church He loves. Also, church leadership needs an appreciation of the sense of loss and grief congregations experience when a pastor leaves. Just as we should not expect someone to quickly "move on" following the death of a close family member, elders should not expect members of their congregations to quickly "move on" following the departure of one with whom they may have had a very close spiritual relationship for many years.

(4) Don't Underestimate the Value of Prayer

This may seem like a given, but prayer doesn't always happen to a large degree amid pastoral transitions, or in an organized way. As leadership coordinates and encourages times of congregational prayer before and during a pastoral search, it involves the congregation in the transition process in a healthy way and helps a church enjoy a key means of God's grace.

(5) Sessions: Strike the Right Balance with the Search Committee

There's a delicate balance that must be sought when it comes to Sessional involvement with search committees. On the one hand, Sessions can provide helpful guidance to search committees as they begin their work. A lack of that guidance on the front end sometimes leaves committees feeling somewhat helpless. The work of search committees would be more efficient if Sessions would formulate pastoral and congregational profiles before committees begin their searches. Search committees then could *begin* with their actual searches and pursue candidates who fit within the general parameters of the profiles established by the Session. This practice also retains the Session in the primary leadership role in the congregation. On the other hand, once a committee has begun its work, its members need to be free to do that work without interference and pressure from the Session.

(6) Search Committees: Don't Look for Mr. Clone— Or Mr. Opposite.

Churches sometimes seek a successor who is just like—or just the opposite of—his predecessor—and both are mistakes. An exact copy of the previous pastor doesn't exist and to pursue him is not only fruitless but keeps the congregation focused on the past instead of moving toward the future. In addition, the other extreme—finding a pastor who is opposite of his predecessor—is problematic as well. While this kind of successor pastor may have gifts his predecessor did not possess, he will be lacking gifts in some areas which are important to the health of the congregation.

The successor pastor needs to possess those ministry strengths of the predecessor which have helped define the ministerial character and approach of the congregation. A congregation *can* benefit from a new pastor who possesses ministerial gifts which the previous pastor did not have. However, the search committee should investigate whether he exercises those gifts in humility, in submission to his fellow elders, and in pursuit of the edification of the body of Christ.

(7) Don't Rush—Be Patient

While it's entirely possible that the search process will be finished relatively quickly and the right man will be called, it's also quite possible that the process will take a considerable length of time. The failure of a search committee to quickly locate a candidate to recommend is not an indication that the committee is failing to do its job. A period of vacancy can actually be God's gift to a congregation. Rushed or pressured decisions are not typically going to be good ones. Sessions as well as congregations can serve search committees well by allowing them to do what they have been charged to do, even if it takes what seems to be a long time. Quality of fit for the new pastor—rather than speed of the search process—should be the desire of the church.

(8) Congregations: Be Realistic in Expectations

Some people will probably leave the church after the pastor leaves—expect it. However, you can also expect that new people will come to the church under the ministry of the new pastor. Also, once the new pastor arrives, members should ask themselves whether they have realistic expectations of him. For example, the new pastor won't know all his members' names when he begins his ministry. He will be different from his predecessor in his temperament, in his mix of spiritual gifts, and in his ministry emphases. If members will allow him to be who God has constituted and gifted him to be, give him an opportunity to minister, and seek to minister with him and to him and his family, it's quite possible that his ministry will be fruitful and long in duration.

(9) Pastors: Honor Each Other

The attitudes of the predecessor and successor pastor are key to a good transition. A humble willingness to honor one's predecessor will help to provide a pastor a good beginning in his new place of ministry. This helps to build up "relational capital" with his church's members and potentially attain a degree of longevity in the congregation. Also, former pastors should not tolerate other people speaking negatively to him about his successor. Be your successor's cheerleader with the congregation.

(10) Remember: Transitions Really Can Go Well!

Conventional wisdom often says otherwise—but transitions are not doomed to failure, even if a popular, long-term pastor is being replaced. Pastoral transitions are hard, but Jesus cares for His church and knows its needs. We can trust Him, His plans for His people, and His presence with us.

About the Author

Larry Gilpin has served as a PCA minister since 1986 with pastorates in Tennessee, Alabama, and Georgia—where he helped prepare his congregation for his departure as a long-term pastor. He has served his current presbytery as its moderator, as chairman of its candidates and credentials committee, and as a member of its shepherding committee, where he assists ministers and congregations dealing with difficult seasons of ministry. He has a heart for mentoring younger ministers, shepherding other pastors, and assisting churches as they deal with pastoral transitions. He is a graduate of Covenant Seminary (M.Div., 1986, D.Min., 2006), where his doctoral dissertation focused on the process of pastoral transitions following the tenure of a long-term pastor. He and his wife, Corley, have been married since 1987 and have two adult daughters.

Endnotes

[1] Philip Collins, "Make Me a Perfect Match," *Crux* 23, no. 3 (1987): 18.

[2] Carolyn Weese and J. Russell Crabtree, *The Elephant in the Boardroom* (San Francisco: Jossey-Bass Publishers, 2004), 5.

[3] Douglas Tilley, "What Are the Factors That Lead Pastors to Change Pastorates?" (D.Min. diss., Covenant Theological Seminary, 2003), 3.

[2] Carolyn Weese and J. Russell Crabtree, *The Elephant in the Boardroom* (San Francisco: Jossey-Bass Publishers, 2004), 5.

[3] Douglas Tilley, "What Are the Factors That Lead Pastors to Change Pastorates?" (D.Min. diss., Covenant Theological Seminary, 2003), 3.

[4] Ibid.

[5] Joshua 4-6.

[6] Joshua 1:1-9.

[7] Numbers 27:18-23.

[8] Richard A. Danielson, "Beating The Odds: Successfully Following A Long-Term Pastor" (D.Min. diss., Asbury Theological Seminary, 2003), 12.

[9] 1 Kings 1:28-48.

[10] 1 Kings 2:3-4.

[11] 1 Kings 1:1-53.

[12] 1 Kings 2:13-46.

[13] 1 Kings 12:1-24.

[14] John 13:33.

[15] John 14:29.

[16] John 14:16, 18; John 16:7.

[17] Matthew 28:18-20; Acts 1:1-11.

[18] 1 Corinthians 2:1,4

[19] Romans 15:4

[20] Douglass astutely notes that this same phenomenon happens when one spouse leaves a marriage for someone else who has the "twenty percent" that their spouse doesn't possess—but not the "eighty per-

cent" of characteristics their spouse did have. The new relationship often fails as well.

CPSIA information can be obtained
at www.ICGtesting.com
Printed in the USA
LVHW011958260720
661581LV00001B/125